For all of the kiddos growing another year cuter, smarter, taller, better...HAPPY BIRTHDAY !!

THIS BOOK BELONGS TO BIRTHDAY KID

____

____

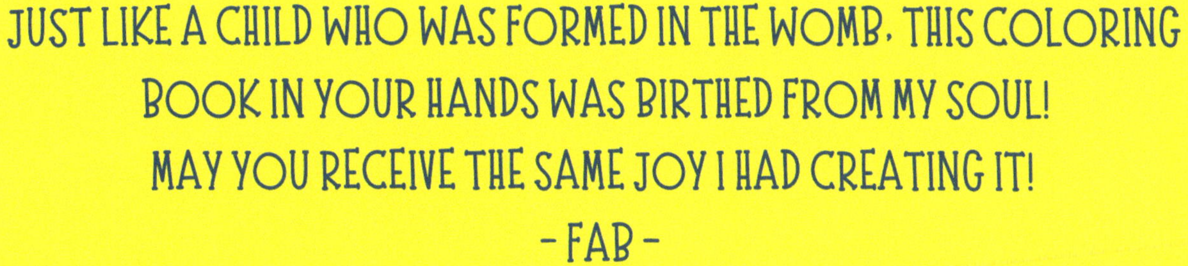

THE BIRTHDAY KID
WWW.FABTHEAUTHOR.COM
FIRST PUBLISHED IN 2023

TO CONTACT THE AUTHOR, PLEASE EMAIL
AUTHORFABLOVE@GMAIL.COM

ISBN 978-1-959035-04-6

Scan the code below to hear a special message from me…
FAB
FaB the Author Message

ALL ABOUT ME

My name is _______________________

I am ____________ years old.

I am from _______________________

I am in Grade: _______________________

My birthday is: _______________________

My Self Portrait!

My top 5 favorite activities are:

1. _______________________

2. _______________________

3. _______________________

4. _______________________

5. _______________________

My favorite food is:

A special note from:

My wish for this year is: _______________________

Come one, come all, today it's all about you!

We line up with excitement,
Just to celebrate you.

You became a
blessing in many
people's lives.

You are loved on
purpose,
The apple of someone's
eye.

Your laughter fills the room with joy. Spending time with you makes it all worthwhile.

You are created full of greatness. A ball of awesomeness inside.

You are
filled with
curiosity.
The world
has much to
be explored.

You are coming
into your own,
New features
not to be
ignored.

Never be afraid to
fail as you will learn
it's a process in life.

You are handsome. You are beautiful. You can be anything. You have the smarts.

You are royalty,
young one,
A King or Queen,
yes YOU are!

Jump out of bed and put on your crown
And shine like a star.

Look in the
mirror
And smile
really big,
Because
today you
are...

THE
BIRTHDAY
KID!
14

HA
BIRT
15

PPY
HDAY

My Birthday

Write and draw how you spent your Birthday. A grown up can help.

Wantmore???
Get your copy of new releases,FaB Swag and more at www.fabtheauthor.com or scan the code below
FAB THE AUTHOR
Tag us & hashtag #readtoogrow for your chance to be featured

Thank ♡ You

I am so grateful to be able to thank all of you who will read this book. Just like a baby who was formed in the womb, this book in your hands was birthed from my soul! May you receive the same joy I had writing it! — FaB

" There is no greater agony than bearing an untold story inside of you."
— Maya Angelou

First and foremost, I thank God Almighty for blessing me with a gift that I can share with the world.

To the love of my life, my spouse, Charles W. Braddy:Thank you for your unconditional love. I thank God for preserving you just for me in His perfect timing. Love you greatly on purpose.

To my children, Branden and Jamauri: You light up my world with laughter and joy. Thank you for being my muse.Love you greatly on purpose.

To my deep roots, my parents, Yvrose and Berny Eliassaint:Thank you for believing in me and pushing me to be my best. Love you greatly on purpose.

To my siblings, Benson, Jutlande, and Bendhie: Thank you for sharing your space and time with me. No matter our shortcomings or downfalls, we are all we have at the end. Love you greatly on purpose.

To my FaB friends & extended family: For every thought and every suggestion you've made in my life and writing journey, no matter how big or small, I appreciate you. Thank you for believing in me. Love you greatly on purpose.

Special thanks to my editor, Starr Balmer-Chore, for accepting the email that would drive me forward in my writing journey. Your expertise and continued guidance is greatly appreciated.

For everyone who has placed a token of wisdom in my life, as I write and create, I thank and love you greatly on purpose. My heart is full as I write this!

FaB

www.ingramcontent.com/pod-product-compliance
Lightning Source LLC
Chambersburg PA
CBHW042143030726
47599CB00002B/605